JOB ESCAPE PLAN

THE 7 STEPS TO BUILD A HOME BUSINESS, QUIT YOUR JOB & ENJOY THE FREEDOM

By

JYOTSNA RAMACHANDRAN

www.jyotsnaramachandran.com

Table of Contents

~

Free Bonus #1

~

As a token of thanks for downloading my book, I would like to give you 100% FREE access to watch the uncut videos of the interviews I did with 7 successful online entrepreneurs - Andy Dew, Alex Genadinik, John Lee Dumas, Nick Loper, Rob Cubbon, Stefan Pylarinos and Steve Scott!

CLICK HERE TO ACCESS

Or go to
http://jyotsnaramachandran.com/freebonus

Free Bonus #2

⌘

If you are too busy to read this book completely, you can't give that excuse anymore! I'm going to give you free access to download the audio book of Job Escape Plan! You can now listen to it while driving or running!

CLICK HERE TO ACCESS

Or go to

http://jyotsnaramachandran.com/freebonus

You can also listen to this audio book for FREE on **Amazon's Audible** and start your FREE 30-day Trial of this audio book membership site.

Audio book on Amazon:
http://www.amazon.com/Job-Escape-Plan-Business-Freedom/dp/B0100NYCIM/

Audio book on Audible:
http://www.audible.com/pd/Business/Job-Escape-Plan-Audiobook/B00ZROOLWW

Introduction

When was the last time you felt super excited about getting ready to go to work? When was the last time your boss showed their appreciation to you for your valuable contribution? Have you ever felt stuck in the wrong job? Have you ever felt like quitting and starting your own dream venture? You are not alone! 87% of the workers are dissatisfied with their jobs and emotionally disconnected from their workplace, according to the latest research conducted by Gallup (a Washington D.C.-based polling organization) in 189 countries on 25 million employees.

This book is written for the millions of people who want to escape their job and do something more meaningful with their life. The Job Escape Plan is a seven step process that will help you start an online business from home, quit your job and live the life of your dreams. This plan will show you the ways to design your ideal lifestyle and develop the means to achieve that in six months or even less.

Just a few years back, I too was working in a boring, mundane job. My friends and family thought that I was doing great, but only I knew that my job title and salary were losing their charm and becoming meaningless. The decision to become an entrepreneur changed my life.

At the time, I didn't have a plan that could smoothly guide me in transitioning from an employee to an entrepreneur. Out of sheer frustration, I quit my job without knowing what to do next. As a result, I spent three years trying my luck with different businesses before I finally discovered and started the ideal business that kindled my passion and supported my dream lifestyle.

Through this book, I am not only sharing my experience as an entrepreneur, but also bringing the combined wisdom of seven other successful online business owners who have taken the bold step of going solo. This book will help you in shortening your learning curve and avoiding the mistakes that we made while quitting our jobs. The strategies shared will help you to be completely prepared before leaving your job so that you taste success from day one.

Each of the seven steps in this book has been written with a purpose. Some steps involve mental work and some involve physical work. Ensure that you read each chapter, take the necessary action and then proceed to the next chapter, so that you don't miss out on any of the pieces of the puzzle!

My husband Girish was working with one of the largest coffee shop chains for more than 12 years. He was very content and comfortable with his job and never thought of becoming an entrepreneur. However, his mindset started changing when he saw my newfound freedom after I started my own venture. He saw that I am able to spend more time with him and our daughter. I am able to take off from work whenever I want without waiting for a boss to sanction my leave. More than anything else,

I am more confident and happier than ever. Girish then followed the exact system I've suggested in this book to discover his passion and quit his job. He is now a Relationship Coach and has started his own company called Human Connect.

I promise you that if Girish and I can do it, you can do it too. By implementing the action points in this simple step-by-step guide, you'll not just be able to quit your job, but also gain the freedom of time, location and money. In less than six months, you'll be able to start a side business that you love, earn more than your day job income and have the flexibility to work from anywhere.

At this point, you have a choice. You can either doubt your ability to succeed and continue doing what you are doing in life, or you can take massive action and create the life of your dreams. You can either flip through this book like just another self-help book or you can treat it like a workbook and take action after every chapter. The choice is yours.

But, it is my humble request that you take control of your life. We all have this one opportunity to live our life to the fullest, spend quality time with the people we love and make a difference to this planet. Why waste our time doing a 9 to 5 job that we hate? I am by no means trying to degrade the work done by people who work for others. As long as they totally love their job and provide value to others, every job is great! But, I do have a serious problem with those who are not happy doing what they are doing.

Don't wait for another year or another month to pass by. Don't wait for your pay raise. Don't wait for that promotion. Now is the time. Get started with the steps involved in starting your home business and saying goodbye to your boss! Now is the time to give yourself the freedom that you were born with. Join me as I take you through your journey from being an employee to an entrepreneur.

Step 1

―――――〜―――――

Get A Reality Check

In this first step, you need to get complete clarity on your current position in life. Only understanding the current scenario will help you in realizing if you need to change it or not. Getting this clarity is crucial as it is going to determine the speed with which you'll take actions in the following chapters. So let's take you through a drill by asking a set of questions that may have a life changing experience for you.

Why am I doing what I'm doing?

To answer this question, you need to press a rewind button in your mind and ask yourself what led you to choose your current profession. Did you decide to become an architect because your best friend enrolled into an architecture school? Did you decide to become an engineer because your 7th grade teacher said that you were good at mathematics? Did you join the hospitality or aviation industry for its glamour factor? Did you become a lawyer because your father has a well established law firm? Or did you decide to become a real estate broker simply because the market was booming?

What factor drove you to choose your current job? Think deeper and try to remember the day when you made the decision. Ask yourself if it was a decision driven by passion for that particular profession or was it an impulsive decision taken due to the situations in your life at that point in time. If your answer is the former, then it's great! But you still need to ask yourself if you continue to have passion for your chosen field or has it worn off over the years. If your answer is the latter, then you most definitely need to course correct your life.

My last job as an employee was with an international fashion brand where I was managing a cluster of retail stores for them. When I asked myself why I joined the retail industry, I realized that I chose to study retail management at my business school as I read about the news of Walmart and Tesco setting up shops in India. It was a big thing for me back then as foreign companies translated to better salaries! Little did I know that I would get bored of my job within five years.

We can either follow our passion or run the rat race. But, we can't do both!

Am I enjoying my job or do I feel sick on Monday mornings?

Do you suffer from Monday morning blues or do you jump out of your bed with excitement? The answer to this question is an indication of whether you like your workplace or not. If your job includes a variety of challenges, you'll find it interesting. If you like your co-workers, you'll look forward to see them after the weekend. If you have a good boss, you'll be excited to learn new things from him/her and contribute to the team. If your company is doing well, you'll have the aspiration to grow along with the company. If your job gives you time to spend with your friends and family, you'll feel more fulfilled.

Do any of the above statements ring a bell to you? On an average, we spend 70% of our waking hours at the work place. We might as well spend this time doing things that we love, rather than living a life of frustration.

Am I using my potential to the fullest?

How do you measure your potential and how do you know if you are using it to your fullest? This happens only when you are using those traits that are unique to you. Each of us was born unique and were blessed with a set of qualities that was unique to us. For example, some people can analyze things in a very unique way. Some can draw, some can sing and some can teach others in a very special way that's unique to them. Only when one identifies this and chooses a profession that utilizes their uniqueness can they use their potential to the fullest.

What happens when a person who is a gifted writer becomes a sales person? Can he do justice to the job? Even if he pushes himself to excel at selling, he will simply continue to be an above average sales person. He cannot be the best in the world. On the other hand, if he chooses to be a copywriter, journalist, blogger, author or screenplay writer, he could possibly use his potential in a much better way and excel in his profession.

Jim Collins, in his book <u>Good to Great</u>, explains this beautifully using the hedgehog concept. He says that if you understand the converging point between what you are deeply passionate about, what you can be the best in the world at and what drives your economic engine, you can identify your sweet spot. In other words, if you find something that you love doing; something you are extremely good at and can also pay you well, your life will be awesome. In most cases, only when you are pursuing a career on your own or running your own business, you'll be able to stick to your sweet spot and delegate the other activities to others.

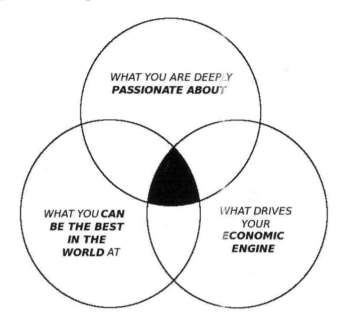

THREE CIRCLES OF THE HEDGEHOG CONCEPT
JIM COLLINS - *GOOD TO GREAT*

What difference is my life making to this world?

We as human beings have various needs to live a fulfilled life. Maslow in his Hierarchy of Needs theory explains this using a pyramid with five levels of needs.

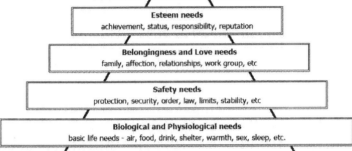

However, in his later years Maslow added one more level to the top of the pyramid above Self-Actualization called Self-Transcendence. He says that even if all the five levels of human needs are satisfied, man still has the highest need of serving others selflessly and making a difference.

Ask yourself how many lives you are touching with your job. In what ways is your job improving the lives of other people? I believe that every job adds some value to others' lives in some way. But what we need to ask ourselves is, "Can I do something else that would touch more lives in a better way?" When you are working for someone else, your employer decides your job profile, its boundaries and its impact. You cannot do much beyond that. But when you are on your own, you are free to do bigger and better things as you wish.

Action Steps

1. Take time to answer the above four questions. It would be better if you write down your answers in a notebook.

   Completing this exercise will give you a clear picture of your current reality. Even if the answer to one of the four questions is in negative, consider it as a wakeup call. This is a call from the universe to pursue something more meaningful and enjoyable in life.

2. You are the creator of your life. In whatever position you are today, it is the result of your past actions. Many people may have influenced you, but the actions taken were your own. Therefore, take 100% responsibility for your life. Take ownership for all the good and bad things that have happened to you so far. This mindset will give you the power to take the action steps to move ahead in life. Stop blaming the people

around you. Be grateful to them as they have helped you in some way in order to get you to where you are today.

Congratulate yourself for answering these difficult questions. The next chapter is going to be a lot easier as you are going to be transported to a dream world!

Step 2

---~---

Design Your Dream Lifestyle

Which is a better option? Having a million dollars in your bank account or living the life of a millionaire? Obviously, the second option! Most people chase money so that they can become rich one day. But what they actually want is to live the lifestyle of a rich person - living in their dream house, going on luxury vacations with family, buying stuff without checking the price tag, having enough time to play golf, traveling in business class, running multiple businesses, donating to charitable causes, etc.

So the idea is not to keep working like a slave throughout your life so that you can retire rich. The idea is to create a dream lifestyle that gives you complete freedom to do what you want, when you want and where you want. And the time to start doing that is NOW! Not after 10 years or 20 years.

So, start thinking of all the things you've always wanted to have and the things you've always wanted to do. To make this activity easy for you, let me take you through some of the things that most of us want in life. Though as human beings, we are all fundamentally the same, the specifics of our dreams and goals vary a lot. Make sure you design your own personal dream lifestyle by the end of this chapter.

Freedom of Money

We all know that money cannot buy everything, but it definitely does make life a lot easier and a lot more enjoyable. What would you do if you had enough money (and then some more) credited to your bank account every month?

I would most definitely buy my dream house first - a 5000 sq ft. beach villa with a beautiful swimming pool, terrace garden, walk-in closet, gym, library and home office. Then I would buy my dream car which is nothing too fancy - just a cute little Volkswagen Beetle. I would take up projects that I love without worrying only about the monetary consequences - like setting up an organic restaurant or starting a New Age school. I would also allocate a part of my income to support causes that are close to my heart.

Freedom of Time

What would you do if you were not forced to work for 10 hours a day? What if your work schedule was flexible and you could decide if you wanted to work that day or not?

I would start pursuing the hobbies that I haven't pursued since high school. I would take classical dance lessons and join a cycling club. I would cook some exotic meals for my family whenever I want to. I would read a new book every week. I would pamper myself at the spa more often. More than anything else, I would spend quality time with my family by doing a lot of fun activities with them. Watching your kids grow is one of the biggest gifts you can give yourself. Spending time with them during their growing years is the most precious thing we can do as parents.

Freedom of Place

What if your work doesn't demand you to report to office every day? What if your clients and vendors don't bug you over the phone? What if you can run profitable businesses by just working for a couple of hours each day from anywhere in the world? I would pack my bag and spend six months a year in a foreign country.

If that sounds too far-fetched, you could still work from your home office and regularly go on all types of vacations - cruise holidays, yoga retreats, gourmet tours, tropical getaways, hiking excursions, etc. You can experience the world with complete freedom - without the pressure of deadlines and a nagging boss! For a moment, stop thinking of "how" this kind of a lifestyle is possible. We will be going in-depth into that area in the following chapters. For now, just let your mind imagine your dream lifestyle. Start designing what your ideal day would look like.

Action Steps

1. Create your list of lifestyle goals

- Pick a good quality journal or paper and write down all the things that you want in your life.

- Be as specific as possible. Instead of writing that you want to go on a holiday every year, write something more specific like "I go on a Mediterranean cruise vacation for 10 days this year. I stay in the Six Senses resort in Maldives for a week next year."

- Write all your goals in present tense. This will trick your sub-conscious mind to believe that these things are already happening in your life. Once you start feeling as if you are living this kind of lifestyle, you will get into the right mindset to attract these things into your life.

- Write a specific date by when you want to achieve each goal. For example, I easily become financially free by December 31, 2015.

- Get into the habit of reading your goals in your lifestyle journal every morning. This routine will motivate you to achieve your goals faster and you'll know if you are on track or not.

2. Create your vision board

This activity may take a couple of hours or more, but it's totally worth it. My life drastically changed after I created my vision board two years back. At that time, I was married for four years and having a child was nowhere in the picture as my husband and I were busy with our careers. But when I was making my vision board, I included a picture of a happy family with a kid. This made me realize what I truly wanted. Nine months later, my daughter was born! Here's my vision board:

- Browse through magazines, newspapers and the internet to find pictures that look close to your dream lifestyle. For example you could include: a girl climbing a mountain, a guy doing vegetable gardening, etc. Look for pictures that resonate with your lifestyle goals.

- Imagine yourself in the picture. See if you can relate to it. Keep the images that make you get excited and discard the rest.

- Take a poster board or a thick paper and start arranging the pictures. You can group together all the travel related photos, fitness related photos, etc.

- Once the board is filled with pictures, start gluing them. Feel free to write inspiring quotations as well.

- Mount your vision board on a wall or keep it on your desk. Ensure you see your board at least once a day and imagine your dream lifestyle.

Step 3

~

Get Into
The Entrepreneur Mindset

Let's face it! 99% of us are not the children of business tycoons. Only 1% of the population inherits a fortune. The rest of us have to create our own destiny. Why do only a tiny fraction of this 99% become self-made millionaires, while the majority of the population continues to be middle class or poor? If you think that the only way the middle class can become rich is by hitting the lottery, then you are absolutely mistaken!

Actually, one-third of lottery winners end up in a serious financial crisis or file for bankruptcy within five years of winning the lottery. This proves that getting the money from somewhere is not the solution. It can provide you the dream lifestyle only for a limited time, until you blow it all up.

Most of the real self-made millionaires have made their money by starting and growing their businesses. There is no other shortcut. They have created a system that will offer products or services to their clients which adds money to their bank accounts month after month. It is no big secret! If the formula to become rich is so obvious and simple, why haven't most people applied it yet? What is stopping you from starting a business? What is preventing you from leading your dream lifestyle? The only answer is - your EMPLOYEE MINDSET.

This fact that I am telling in your face may be hard to digest, but we cannot proceed to the "HOW" of this book without getting this straight. Only when you shift your mindset to think like an entrepreneur will you be able to take action and attract opportunities in your life. In this chapter, let's look at the most common excuses that are stopping you from making the transition from an employee to an entrepreneur.

Excuse #1: It's too risky to quit my job

This would have been a valid excuse 10 years back before we all witnessed the recession in 2008, but not anymore. We all saw how millions of people lost their jobs and became unemployed overnight. Job security is a myth. The biggest risk you can take in life is to hand over the steering wheel of your life to your employer.

When you totally depend on your employer for your monthly salary, you are literally at the mercy of the company. Even if you are one of the top performers in your company, there could be a lot of external factors that can put your job at risk. The company's shares may go down in the stock market due to some negative PR and they may have to downsize. The management policies of the company may change due to their collaboration with a foreign partner. Or you may just end up fighting with your boss over a trivial issue and get fired! Anything is possible.

On the other hand, if you are an entrepreneur, you take total control over your life. You can set targets for your business and get the resources to achieve it. If you can see some great opportunities coming up in your industry, you can take the action steps that can double or triple your business. You need not wait for a pay raise! If you foresee some challenges in the market, you can quickly take the necessary steps to diversify your portfolio and safeguard your business.

You need not wait till your sales go down. When you are an employee, your performance will directly depend on the support you receive from the other departments like marketing, finance, human resources, etc. When you are an entrepreneur, you handle all these departments. This gives you total freedom and control over how you want your business to grow.

Excuse #2: Starting a business needs a huge investment

If you are planning to set up a manufacturing unit or a retail store, it's going to cost you lots of money. For most normal people like you and me, who save very little money, these kinds of high investment businesses could be too far-fetched. But, not all businesses need a huge investment. This is the reason why I am a huge fan of online businesses. For most of the internet based businesses, all you need is a laptop and an internet connection to start off.

I started my Kindle Publishing business with an initial investment of $100 which went towards creating my first Kindle ebook. I then started publishing more and more books from the profits I made from the sales of the book.

If you plan to start a blog, all you need to spend for is a domain name ($10), a hosting service ($6 per month), a logo (done on fiverr.com for $5) and a good website (WordPress theme bought on themeforest.com for $58). A YouTube channel can be started using your iPhone camera. Once you start making some profits, you can invest in a DSLR ($500), microphone ($25) and lights ($100) to set up a home studio. You pretty much need the same kind of investment for creating online courses on Udemy.com.

I am not saying that you can become a millionaire by investing just $100 into your online business. But I am suggesting that you just need a small amount to start off. Selling physical products on Amazon.com is a very lucrative business opportunity. You may have to invest a $1000 on this business model. But even that is much less than the money people invest into their offline businesses.

Excuse #3: I need to hire employees

It is true that you cannot scale up any business without the help of other people. But the good news is that the people who are going to help you don't have to be your employees! You don't have to recruit a team of MBAs to run your start-up venture. In fact, I highly recommend that you do not recruit any employees when you start your business.

Until you become familiar with the various processes in your business, do everything yourself. Then divide the tasks into critical tasks that only you can do, important tasks that you cannot do and the routine tasks that anyone can do. Spend your precious time doing only the critical tasks like making business decisions.

The important tasks could need a specialist like a copywriter or designer. You can outsource these project-based tasks as needed when you have a specific need.

You can then have the routine tasks like admin work, customer service, marketing, etc., done by virtual assistants. These assistants work with you on a regular basis to perform the everyday tasks and you pay them for the exact amount of work they do.

For my Kindle Publishing business, I spend my time deciding the book topics to publish, collaborating with authors and updating myself with the latest developments in the industry. I outsource my book writing, editing, cover designing, audio book recording etc., to specialists on odesk.com, elance.com or fiverr.com. My team of virtual assistants (whom I've never met!) take care of promoting the books, scheduling activities, formatting the books etc.

I therefore don't have to pay monthly salaries to anyone. I started off by doing everything myself. As the business grew, I started outsourcing the tasks to freelancers who are helping me grow my business faster.

Excuse #4: I need to rent an office space

Have you ever wondered why companies have offices? An office gives a formal structure to efficiently manage the work of the employees. The other purpose of an office is to serve as an identity for the company and a place to meet the clients.

When your business is online, you don't need either! You create a system to manage your virtual assistants who live in different parts of the world. You can manage their work using some cool apps like Trello or Basecamp. Your online presence is your company's identity and your clients meet you on the internet. Some of the top internet marketers like Brendon Burchard and Jeff Walker who make millions of dollars online still work from their home offices.

All you need is a quiet corner at home to work on your online business. Unless you want to impress your neighbor or you hate to spend time at home, a swanky office is not required. This is one of the main reasons why starting an online business is perfect for people who are working. You can be an employee at work and an entrepreneur when you get back home to work on your business. The transition will be so smooth that people around you will barely notice!

Excuse #5: I am too young and don't have the experience

If you are working somewhere and feel that you need to gain more experience in that industry before you start you own venture, please note that this experience would only help you become an employee. You cannot learn to drive a car by sitting on the passenger's seat and observing the driver.

You need to sit on the driver's seat, with an experienced driver sitting next to you, and just start driving! This is exactly what we'll be discussing in Step 5 of the process - how to prepare yourself in your chosen line of business. Having said that, you cannot spend your whole life preparing. You just need to get your basics right and get started. You can keep improving yourself along the way. Even the so-called experienced people need to keep upgrading themselves to stay relevant in this fast changing world.

I believe that every skill is learnable. So don't waste anymore time. The more the time you spend as an employee, the more you are postponing your freedom. The value you are going to deliver to your customers through your business matters. Age is irrelevant.

Excuse #6: I am too old to start from scratch

Again, age is irrelevant. You may be an expert in what you are doing, but when you start your business you need to approach it with an open mind. You'll have to empty your glass. Only then you'll be receptive to learning new things.

Research shows that our brain cells keep increasing as we age. But the only reason why older people find it difficult to learn new things is because of their conditioned mindset. If you are willing to unlearn, learning a new skill will be a cake walk.

Another mind block that I see with older people is their aversion to technology. You need not be a tech geek to start an online business! If you are savvy enough to send emails and check your Facebook account, you are good to go. The other complex technology related work can be outsourced to freelancers on elance.com!

Excuse #7: I don't know what business to start

This is where most people get stuck before they start a business. They feel that they are good at nothing and there is too much competition in the market for everything. The beauty of the internet is that you could be doing the most peculiar type of business like selling goggles for dogs and still be making lots of money! As the internet allows you to target a global market, you'll find people interested in your niche from different parts of the world and they'll make a sizeable set of clients to make your business viable.

There are people who start multiple businesses and finally fail at everything as they are not sure what business to focus on. The secret sauce to success is to choose one business, grow it, automate it and then move to the next one. The next chapter is dedicated towards finding your profitable niche, by the end of which you'll be sure of what business are you going to start. But before we get there, let's do some important homework.

Action Steps

1. Get clarity on your "WHY"

Simon Sinek, in his book "Start with Why", talks about the differences between successful companies like Apple and the others. He says that most businesses know WHAT to do and some of them even know HOW to do it, but very few of them know WHY they do it.

When you start with why, you'll be able to communicate effectively to all the people who believe in what you believe, thereby making them your raving fans, rather than just your customers.

In this exercise, let's get clarity on why are you starting your online business from home. This will not just help you market your product to like-minded people, but also give you the motivation to reach your goals on days when you feel like quitting.

Once you know your "why," it becomes much easier to know your "what" in Step 4 and your "how" in Step 5.

For me, the reasons for starting my Kindle publishing business were the following:

- Ability to work from home and spend more time with my newborn daughter.
- Enjoy the freedom of being my own boss.
- Become financially free by the time my daughter starts school.
- Publish ebooks that make a difference in people's lives.

- Become a role model for others who seek freedom from their jobs and inspire them through my work.

Start writing down your WHY's.

2. Read positive affirmations every morning

Our subconscious mind needs to be rewired to think like a successful entrepreneur even before we start a business. If you are an employee and are going to embark in this new, unfamiliar path, it's all the more important to reinforce positive thoughts on a regular basis.

This will help in suppressing the self-doubts and fears associated with starting your business and keep you in a positive frame of mind to achieve your goals. Read this list of business-specific affirmations every morning:

- My life is in my hands. I take 100% responsibility for all the things that happen in my life.
- I have the entrepreneurial mindset. I am my own boss.

- I have the ability to convert any idea into a successful business. I have the Midas touch.
- I am extremely good at managing people and getting my work done from them.
- I am excellent at managing my finances. I save and invest in my business wisely.
- I am a very good time manager. I plan my day well and balance my professional and personal life very well.
- I attract great clients who love me and my business.
- Wonderful business opportunities keep coming my way and I create multiple income streams.
- I earn enough passive income to support my desired lifestyle.
- Every day I am moving one step closer to my financial freedom by taking massive action.
- I touch millions of lives and create a positive impact in this world through my business ventures.

Step 4

Choose The Perfect Niche For You

Selecting the right niche is one of the most critical steps in starting your business. I recommend people to do this by following one of the two routes:

The Interest Route

Please refer to the hedgehog concept that we discussed in Step 1. It says that your sweet spot lies in an area that you are very good at, that has a good market potential and you also love doing it. You can identify this niche by asking yourself questions like:

- What are the topics that I've always been passionate about?
- What kind of books and magazines do I keep reading?
- What kind of TV shows and YouTube videos do I often watch?
- People come to me for advice on what kind of topics?
- In what areas do I always end up helping people?
- When I am with friends or at a party, what kind of conversations grabs my attention?
- What kind of email newsletters have I subscribed to?
- Can I think of a few people who have succeeded in this industry?

This exercise will give you some clarity on what industry and niche is right for you. Just remember that everyone is good at something. Self-doubt is the number one reason that stops people from chasing their dreams. Even if you feel that you are good at nothing, you will still have special interests in some areas and you may be better than many people in that area. You may not be the best in the world in that niche yet, but you can become one with continuous effort.

The Market Route

Another way to identify a niche is to look for markets that you are a part of or you are very familiar with. If you are associated with certain groups of people, the chances of you understanding their pain points is much better. When you can think by placing yourself in your customer's shoes, you'll be able to come up with solutions that the market has been waiting for.

For example, if you are a mother and you are constantly in touch with other mothers, you'll be able to relate to the problems faced by this market segment well. For example, putting infants and toddlers to sleep at night could be a nightmare for moms. You could write a book on this based on your experience, or you could interview other moms who have dealt with the problem successfully and release it as a DVD or you can market innovative sleep inducing products like sleep positioners, lullaby CDs, vibrating mattresses, slumber sound machines, baby hammocks, etc.

If you are a member of a trekking club, think of all the problems trekkers face and come up with solutions for them. Don't worry about how you are going to create these products and reach out to your target market. We'll be going into the "how" in the next step.

Action Steps

1. Make an exhaustive list of all your interests that you can think of. Do not filter the ideas in your mind. Just keep writing down everything that comes to your mind. Spend 15 minutes doing this.

2. Make another list of all the groups that you are a part of: health/sports/leisure clubs, charity organizations, cultural associations, religious groups, business networks, college alumni associations, etc. Out of these groups, choose

one that you have the greatest affinity to. Write down all the common problems faced by the members of this group and the business ideas that provide a solution.

3. Now go through each area of interest/business idea and check if they meet the three criteria described in the hedgehog concept: something that you love doing, something you are extremely good at and something that can also pay you well.

4. Check the online market potential of your niche by doing some keyword research to estimate the search traffic for topics in your niche. Google Keyword Planner and Market Samurai are great keyword research tools.

5. You may also be confused because you may have multiple interests and may be good at multiple things. That's awesome! Just make a note of the top three most profitable niches that you would like to consider.

In the next chapter you'll get more clarity on which one is best for you. You'll see how any idea or niche can be taken to an online platform and converted into a profitable business.

Step 5

Choose the Best Online Business Platform For You

Starting an online business is the best way to start a business while you are still working for an employer. You can quietly work on your side hustle for a couple of hours a day and it won't affect your other daily activities in any way. It is the safest, easiest and fastest way to create a side income that'll soon become more than your full-time income. Once you have this comfort cushion, you can get ready to leave your job!

The entire world is buying online! Even if you already own an offline business, I would highly recommend you to also have an online presence. I see so many business owners who look more miserable than their employees because of poor systems, long hours of work, irritated clients, constant phone calls and delayed payments from clients. They can avoid most of these problems if they take their business online. An internet-based business is ideal for those who want a dream lifestyle and want complete freedom of time, place and money.

Let me demonstrate this concept with a couple of examples.

If you've chosen home decor as the niche you want to start your business in, these are the typical traditional ways of starting a business in this niche:

- Becoming an interior designer for homes.
- Setting up a retail store that sells home furnishings, furniture, art work, etc.
- Manufacturing your own brand of home decor products and selling them through retail chains like Bed, Bath & Beyond.

- Starting a magazine on home decor.
- Writing a book on home decor and getting it published through a publishing house.
- Hosting a TV show on home interior makeovers.

Do any of the above business ideas look easy? All of them involve huge investment of your time and money. For a person who is working in a day job and hasn't saved enough to quit his/her job, these business ideas will sound like fairy tale. This is the reason why 95% of the people continue to be employees for the rest of their lives. Though they would love to follow their passion, they do not have a plan to escape their job.

Let's now see some of the online business ideas for a person who loves home decor:

- Having a blog that talks about the latest trends and gives expert tips on interior design. The blog would make money by recommending good products (affiliate marketing) as well as by featuring ads.
- Creating a software or a mobile app for DIY interior design. People can drag and drop

design elements in 3D rooms where the dimensions can be customized.

- Writing a series of books on home decor and self-publishing on Kindle.
- Starting a YouTube channel that shows home interior makeovers.
- Sourcing home decor products from manufacturers, branding them and selling them through online retailers like Amazon.
- Creating online video courses on interior design and selling the courses though Udemy.com.

Can you see the difference? The same products and services can be offered through an online platform by investing a small fraction of the time and money invested in an offline business.

The best part of running an online business is the passive income it offers. You put in your hard work once and reap the benefits for the rest of your life! You literally earn while you sleep. By creating an online course once, you'll be able to earn every time someone purchases the course.

Compare this with teaching this to students face to face. Even if you work for the most prestigious college, you'll have to trade your time for money. You'll get paid only if you are physically present for your lecture. Whereas if your course is online, you could be on a vacation in Bali and a student from Italy would be learning from you. How cool is that!

A friend of mine is a celebrity fitness trainer in India. He is the most sought after trainer as he's given the enviable six pack abs to many movie stars. He has come a long way since his days as an employee at a local gym. He is now self-employed and enjoys the freedom of working when he wants and with whom he wants.

When I caught up with him recently, I told him that though his career is going great, he could be doing a lot better if he leveraged himself by having an online presence. At first he was very skeptical about the idea of even having a website because he has so many good clients. But when we discussed it further, he realized that he can work for only a certain number of hours a day.

This limitation put an upper ceiling to the amount of money he can earn and the number of people he can train. Also, he is not able to work when he is travelling or on days when he's not feeling well. On the other hand, if he starts an online business, he can do one or more of the following:

- Reach out to his followers through his fitness blog.
- Create his own personal brand of health supplements, yoga mats, weights, workout clothes, etc., and sell them through online retailers.
- Recommend the best gyms, fitness equipment, diet programs and earn as an affiliate partner.
- Create workout DVDs and sell them through online stores.
- Create online video courses for various fitness goals. This would be perfect for people who want his guidance but can't afford his personal training.
- Start a podcast where he can interview celebrities and they can share their fitness secrets with his followers.

All the above online platforms will generate passive income which will transform my friend from a self-employed professional to an entrepreneur. He will also be able to serve more people, rather than restricting himself to a limited number of clients. More than anything else, he'll be able to pass on his legacy to the next generation by creating online products.

Now let's look at some of the real life success stories of people who have taken the online route and crushing it big time! I had the privilege of interviewing these successful online entrepreneurs who have chosen 7 different online platforms to establish authority in their chosen niche.

1. Blogging

Blogging is the most common way to start your online brand. With the advent of WordPress, this has become extremely easy. You can share your message in an instant with the world. You can build a following by consistently writing high quality blog posts, which connects you with your reader. These readers can later be converted into loyal customers. Learn some blogging tips from the famous blogger Nick Loper.

Interview with Nick Loper
(www.sidehustlenation.com)

Me: It could a big challenge to decide the niche one has to focus on in their blog. Can you suggest some ways to do identify the perfect niche?

Nick: The blog in itself could be a pretty bad business because it is pretty hard to make money with just the blog. But, if you think of the blog as a content marketing platform for some greater business, it would make more sense. You have to figure out what you are going to sell behind the blog. Think about how it's going to make money. My hourly rate from blogging is not very much. But, its fun, a very creative outlet and I enjoy writing!

Me: *So you mean that the blog in itself cannot be a business, but it has to be supporting a main business?*

Nick: It definitely can be, but it takes huge amounts of traffic for the blog to stand alone on its own. For example the "Pinch of Yum" blog (http://pinchofyum.com/) has done very well. They make money by advertising, through product sales by selling their books and they have also branched out by teaching others how to run a successful food blog. So, to monetize just with advertising takes a ton of traffic.

Me: *Which is the best way to monetize a blog? Having ads using Google Adsense, promoting other products as an affiliate or creating your own products or services? For Google Adsense to work, you'll need tons of traffic, like probably a food blog. But for the other kinds of blogs, which is the best method?*

Nick: For people who are starting, I would say – a service. You can offer something like a podcast editing help or a monthly social media management packages or something along those lines. It would be a bonus if it has a recurring element to it where you can keep getting paid over and over again.

I spoke to a guy who has a service called www.ghostblogwriters.com. His company has a blog that talks about the value of blogging, the value of content marketing etc., because they want to sell more people on the ghost blogging service they have. That's a good way to go about it.

Me: *So, a person shouldn't start a blog just based on their passion, right? They should be good at something and offer that as a service on their website.*

Nick: Yes, but you should be interested in the topic because you'll need to create content. I started a handful of sites, one of them was a wine site. I didn't know anything about the topic and I didn't really care about it. It was a horrible site! So, you need to at least have interest in the subject matter, otherwise it's going to be difficult to keep pushing it forward.

Me: Blogging is an activity where you need to consistently produce very high quality content. How do you come up with interesting topics?

Nick: I go through spurts. Sometimes I feel I've said everything I can ever say on this topic and don't know what I am going to write about. Sometimes I just come up with 10 different ideas! So, before you start if you can come up with 50 potential article ideas, it's a signal that there's probably enough to keep going. I started with doing two posts a week, which became too much on the writing side. So I narrowed it to one post a week.

Me: How did Side Hustle Nation start Nick? Was it a part of another business or was it started as a passion to help other side-hustlers?

Nick: I've been following Pat Flynn and Chris Ducker. Chris told me that I should build my personal brand. At that point, I was already blogging for four years and never had a consistent branding. All the entrepreneurial projects I've been working on fell under the Side Hustle umbrella, so I liked the idea. It's been almost two years since I started Side Hustle Nation.

Me: When you started, choosing a domain name would've been an important decision. For example, Chris Ducker's domain name is chrisducker.com. Why didn't you start with nickloper.com, but instead went for a domain name that resonates with the topic?

Nick: That's a great question! I actually did start with nickloper.com back in 2009. When I went through this rebranding decision, there was a lot of debate about that. A lot of people like Chris were switching from a domain like virtual business lifestyle to their name. Back then, no one was reading my personal blog. So my theory was that if I have a very clear domain name, it would be easy to market and spread the word around.

Me: You give a lot of importance to lead generation. In every page of your blog, there are 3-4 buttons for people to click and opt-in for the free content you provide. Which have been the best lead magnets that have worked for you?

Nick: I've tried a few. When I started, I just had one. I gave away the Side Hustle Library - the snippets from some of my favorite business books. That did okay, but it wasn't really related to the rest of the content. So, I switched it to giving the fastest ways to make money outside your day job. That performed a little better. But what has really driven the email list growth is the podcast. I've been creating episode specific opt-in offers that give the tactics discussed in the episode.

Me: Your Side Hustle Nation Show has crossed 100 episodes! A common trend that I'm noticing now is that a lot of bloggers are moving to podcasting. Do you think people have changed the way they consume content?

Nick: I was excited about the podcast so that I can try something new. It has grown so much faster than the blog, because it's less competitive. I also think that a listener is a lot more valuable than a reader. If someone is going to spend half an hour with you plugged into their ear buds, that's a deeper relationship than someone who just scans your blog post for two minutes. So, starting a podcast was a strategic move! It's also great for networking. It gives me an excuse to talk to some awesome people through my podcast.

Me: Why do you think the competition in podcasting is less? Is it difficult to set up a home studio?

Nick: My home studio is just my USB mic. Podcasting just needs an extra effort which many people do not put in.

Me: I am a student of your Udemy course and I've also read your books. Do you think all bloggers should eventually experiment with other platforms?

Nick: Yes, absolutely! You should see where else you can reach your target customer. But, it's good to do one thing at a time. Amazon Kindle would make a lot to sense to someone who is starting out because you can potentially reach millions of customers. You can then bring the customers to your blog by offering something for free inside your book.

Me: People who want to start a blog either feel that there is no market for their topic or they feel that the market is so huge that they'll get lost in the competition. Where do they strike a balance?

Nick: It's better to have a small piece of the big market, rather than have a big piece of a non-existing market. 100% of zero is still zero, right? The point of differentiation is the most important thing. If you plan to start an entrepreneurship interview podcast, ask yourself how you are going to be different from Entrepreneur on Fire. Your personality and your unique background and experience can bring in that differentiating factor. For example, a person I am coaching wants to create a travel hacking app, but from a super analytical engineer's perspective. That's how he is planning to stand out in a competitive space.

Me: Is there a way to find out the size of the market?

Nick: You can look at keyword traffic estimates. You can check out www.compete.com or www.similarweb.com to find out the traffic, social profiles etc., of the competitors. You can look at other blogs in that space, start following them, sign up to their email list, see how they are making money and then spin your idea to make it slightly different from the others. The Tropical MBA podcast has this business idea framework called Rip, Pivot, Jam, where you take somebody else's idea, pivot it to a new market by adding a twist and then start working on it. It doesn't need to be something completely original.

2. Podcasting

A podcast is a channel that offers voice content to its listeners. This medium is gaining huge popularity in the last few years as more and more people like to consume content on the go. This has the potential to make your voice be heard across the world. Listen to how you can start your podcast from the horse's mouth!

Interview with John Lee Dumas
(www.entrepreneuronfire.com)

Me: I see a lot of bloggers moving into podcasting. What's the reason for this trend?

JLD: Bloggers are already producing content. They are content producers. Now, they are thinking why not take this content that they've already produced and repurpose it in a different medium. There's a whole set of people who read blogs. But there's a whole set of other people who love listening to audio content while driving, or while they are at the gym! So, here's an opportunity to capture a larger audience via podcast by making your content available on iTunes, Stitcher, Sound Cloud, etc.

iTunes has over 525 million active users, which is double the population of the United States and half the population of India! So if you are producing content on a blog, why not put it in front of this massive audience that may want to be consuming it?

Me: How does it work? Once I produce content on my podcast, should I individually go and submit it to iTunes, Stitcher and the other places?

JLD: What's amazing about podcasting it that it works exactly like how you produce content on a blog. Through RSS (Really Simple Syndication), it gets instantly and automatically sent to all those who have subscribed to your RSS feed. It's the exact same thing with podcasting. When you submit your podcast, it is syndicated to all these directories automatically. So, you submit your podcast only one time to iTunes, only one time to Sound Cloud, only one time to Stitcher and then every time you publish a podcast, it gets syndicated to all these directories automatically.

Me: *Wow! That makes life so simple. Your podcast Entrepreneur on Fire has a huge following of entrepreneurs. Entrepreneurs are a tribe who love to keep learning new stuff. But, would podcasting work for a lawyer, architect or chef?*

JLD: Yes, entrepreneurs are a small percentage of the population. Let's look at traditional industries. They are way behind times. My brother-in-law is a real estate broker. He launched a podcast where he interviews successful real estate brokers from across the world and finds out the tools and tactics that have worked for them. His market used to be his neighborhood, but now his audience is the world! I have a friend who's a dentist. In his podcast, he teaches other dentists how to franchise their business. So if you belong to a traditional industry and you start a podcast, you have that first mover's advantage. You'll be in the top 1% in that industry and will become the leader of the pack.

Me: *That's amazing! To do what nobody else in your industry is doing. And by the time they follow you, your business would've sky-rocketed!*

JLD: Let me use Entrepreneur on Fire as an example. When I launched it, it was the first seven days a week podcast. The other entrepreneur shows were at most once a week or twice a month. I was one of the first movers to dig into interview podcasts. That's probably why when you wanted to interview someone from the podcasting industry, I was the first person to come to your mind. So, I've kind of established myself as an authority figure which was possible by being a first mover.

Me: John, tell me your secret. Do you actually interview a person every day or do you batch process your work?

JLD: I batch process to the nth degree. On Tuesdays, I do eight interviews, one every hour. It's a long eight hours where I put my heart and soul into it. Once I quash this day, I know I have six days to recover and also focus on other areas of my business. I not only record the interviews, but I also edit all of them myself. I've developed a great system where I just take 5-7 minutes to edit an episode. I do have three virtual assistants who take a lot of things off my plate. They take care of activities like submitting the podcast to iTunes. But the core interviewing for Entrepreneur on Fire is done by me. It's my baby. Wednesdays are my "everything else" days. I do interviews like this one, I have my mastermind calls, I schedule my podcast interviews, etc. On Mondays, Thursdays and Fridays my calendar is empty. That's my personal time.

Me: Thanks for sharing your productivity tip John! I can see your beautiful mic there, which a person who is starting out may not be able to afford. What's the bare minimum that's required to start a podcast?

JLD: I'll give it to you! The bare minimum you need is some kind of computer, tablet or even a smart phone would do. That's step number one. Step two is a microphone. I'll recommend the two best value microphones. These are low cost yet high quality and can produce really good sounding podcasts. It's called the Logitech ClearChat. It's a $30 headset mic. One step above that which I highly recommend is the Audio-Technica ATR 2100. It's a dynamic microphone and costs $60. It's just amazing. It'll take your audio quality from a 6 in Logitech to an 8.5. My girlfriend uses this for her podcast. The third microphone which I want to mention is the Heil Sound PR40. That's the one I'm using. It's $330, a little expensive, but it's an excellent podcast quality mic. Step three is recording and editing software. I'd recommend Adobe Audition, which costs $20 per month. You can also get Audacity or Garage Band which are completely free. If you want to record calls over Skype, you can use eCamm Call Recorder for Mac or Pamela for PC.

Me: If a person is not yet an expert in his/her industry, how do they spread the word around about their new podcast?

John: Podcasting is perfect for people who are not experts in their industries as well as people who are already experts. When I launched I had no expertise in entrepreneurship. I had no podcasting experience. But, I was able to ask great entrepreneurs to come on my show like Tim Ferriss, Barbara Corcoran, Gary Vaynerchuk. I told them that I have a podcast that has a legit listenership. It's not huge now but it's growing. I asked, "Would you spend 25 minutes on a call over Skype with me?" And they agreed. I didn't have the expertise, I just had the questions. They brought in the expertise and the value. But it happened via my show. As soon as the episode goes live, the first email goes to that day's guest. I make it very easy for them to share it with their audience. It's a great value for their audience too. They then check out what's this interview show about and if they find the seven days a week concept cool, they become our subscribers!

Me: *Yours is predominantly an interview podcast, but there are some great Q & A podcasts as well like the ones hosted by Steve Scott and Pat Flynn. Which would be a better option for someone starting out?*

John: When you start out, you'll neither have too many followers nor would you have much knowledge. Therefore, Q & A shows would not work, as you'll be saying that's a good question, but will not have any answers to give! Over time when you build your expertise and get to the level of Pat Flynn or where I am now, you'll have some knowledge to share. I must mention that I am soon coming up with a JLD Q & A show which I'm really looking forward to. I am going to have weekend jam sessions, where I'll have two episodes on Saturday and Sunday.

Me: That'll definitely add a lot of value to your followers! Can you suggest some ways to monetize a podcast?

John: Just like blogging, you need to provide value consistently, for free, to build the audience. I started doing that with Entrepreneur on Fire from the very beginning. After a point, my audience started sharing with me their troubles and pain points. This was the opportunity for me to create the solution in the form of a product or service or a community. Now I've done that with Fire Nation Elite mastermind where I have 100 people paying me $200 a month to be a part of the membership mastermind. For two years, I also did one-on-one coaching where I would mentor four mentees a month and they paid me $2000 per month. I have two sponsors for every show. I didn't have any sponsors when I started, but I got them when I built an audience that the sponsors wanted to be in front of. Now Entrepreneur on Fire generates $70000 a month on sponsorship revenue alone. This is possible because it's a daily show. That's the kind of monetization you can see when your show becomes successful.

Me: One has to be consistent over a period of time. Nothing happens overnight, right?

John: Yes. Consistency can be three times a week or even once a week. Your audience should trust you and you reward their trust with consistency. Then you get to a point where you can create products and services for them. We train our students of Podcaster's Paradise, which is the #1 podcasting community in the world. We have 2200 members in it and it has generated $2.2 million of revenue since we launched in Oct 2013. We have 200 video tutorials, a private Facebook group, monthly webinars with Tim Ferriss, Gary Vaynerchuk, Pat Flynn, etc., and many incredible things!

Me: That's wonderful! I am sure you wouldn't have done all this if you hadn't offered lots of value up front through your free Podcast and Webinar courses.

John: That's right. If you give away enough value for free and if a person ever decides that he's going to invest in a course, they would go to a person they already know they can trust.

3. YouTube

You can shoot some great videos to reach out to people who prefer the visual medium. YouTube is the second largest search engine after Google and offers you a great platform to educate, inspire and entertain your followers through videos. Read the interview to find out how Stefan Pylarinos has been able to build an online business empire by using YouTube.

Interview with Stefan Pylarinos
(www.projectlifemastery.com)

Me: *A person who is working full time faces two challenges: they don't have too much time; neither do they have too much money to invest. So, in that scenario, which would be the best business to start off with?*

Stefan: That's a great question and of course, my answer is a little bit biased because as you know, I'm passionate about Kindle publishing and I've seen the freedom and the opportunity that it's created for people. It's very beneficial for a lot of people who don't have the time or the money necessary to do it. Kindle publishing is a way for people to get started making money online without having to know a lot of technical stuff because I found that a lot of the other ways of making money require a lot of knowledge about internet marketing, copywriting, web design, WordPress, all these sort of things that I think intimidate a lot of people. Whereas for Kindle publishing, I have members of my course from the age of 15-16 years to up to 70 years old. So I like Kindle publishing for the ease and the simplicity of it, as well as the speed in which you can start to immediately make money. You can start making money in a few weeks from now and I like it just because there's not much startup expense. Amazon physical products do cost maybe a couple of thousand dollars to get started, whereas with Kindle publishing, you can do it for less than a hundred dollars, and it doesn't require much of your time either.

Me: Right, I think I agree because that's how I also started, and only now I'm looking at the other avenues. One thing I've seen you doing differently from other online entrepreneurs is the way you've used YouTube to your advantage. You keep producing such amazing video content with great consistency and speed. How do you do that?

Stefan: I think YouTube is very powerful because a lot of the blogs out there are just written content, and it's very hard to stand out and differentiate yourself with just written content. People are consuming information in different ways - they're listening to podcasts, they're watching videos, and I just realized that I wanted to take advantage of the trend. I wanted to be different from the typical bloggers out there, and I felt that by using YouTube I can develop a deeper relationship and connect with people. I'm just constantly focused on adding value in everything that I put out. I always make sure that I'm in the best state that I could possibly be in when I'm shooting the videos and I keep asking myself how can I serve the people who are watching my channel or buying my products. I think by me sharing my life and being so open, people are able to connect on a much deeper level. Some people say that my videos have saved their life. They were suicidal, were on depressants and drugs and by watching my videos they've changed their lives. When the effect is so profound, they become my raving fans. This relationship, trust and goodwill that I've established just by putting myself out there has helped me a lot.

Me: *You are right. When you're face to face with your audience, and you're looking into their eyes and talking, it makes a lot of difference.*

Stefan: I think the key thing for me has just been not being a perfectionist. If you look back at my videos of 2012, they are horrible compared to what they are today. The quality, my speaking ability and my confidence have evolved. When I first started, I was a little bit self-conscious. I didn't like the way that I looked or the way that I sounded. But now I'm able to disassociate myself from that and just ask myself "will this help someone?" and if this helps one person, then it's worth publishing. So I don't really have too high of standards by trying to be a perfectionist, I just record to the best of my ability and then, just put it out there.

Me: *Wow, I think self-doubt is something that stops a lot of people, especially to come in front of the camera, because it could be intimidating but I think the moment* *you change your mind set to helping someone, rather than looking good, I think a lot of things can be achieved! What is the kind of equipment you would suggest somebody should have to record videos?*

Stefan: I actually don't think you need fancy equipment. I just started with a little digital camera that I had. I didn't even have a tripod, I just had a stack of books! My camera equipment now costs a couple of thousand dollars, but I didn't need that to get started. I think in many ways, the more raw the video is, the more real it is, people can relate to it a lot more. I even use my iPhone at times and I found that's been pretty successful for me. Just get the bare minimum of what you need to get started, and then as you start making money, then you can invest more into better equipment.

Me: So how did you actually manage to bring traffic to your channel? Because it's great to upload the videos, but people should find your videos on YouTube, right?

Stefan: To be honest with you, I think there's definitely a lot more that I can do. Until recently, I've never paid for advertising or traffic. I knew a little bit about how YouTube works. For example, if you put in the keywords that people are searching for, they're going to find your video. When I first started, I was just putting out content and I would share it just on my Facebook and Twitter. For example, my first videos in 2012 got around five views, and only from my friends! The challenge with YouTube and blogging is that you don't get immediate results. Eventually because I kept putting out more and more content, my YouTube channel started growing organically. If your content is good, people will like it and share it which will give you more exposure. Now, all my videos get over 1,000-2,000 views. I have over 34,000 people that have subscribed. So over time, it has a snowball effect, but at the beginning it was very slow.

Me: So one cannot expect some overnight miracles to happen on YouTube right?

Stefan: Right. Nonetheless, I think some people are able to because they leverage an email list. Even if you don't have an email list of your own, you can promote yourself on other people's blogs or YouTube channels. If you go on another guy's podcast and if his audience likes you, then obviously, they're going to subscribe to you as well.

Me: *When someone clicks on the ad that comes on your YouTube video, you get paid, right? Is this ad revenue substantial?*

Stefan: In the last 2-3 years, my videos have almost 2 million views, but I just make $400-500 per month from YouTube ads.

Me: *In spite of having so many views?*

Stefan: Yeah, that's because some videos make more money than others based on what advertisers are bidding for. For example, the ad revenue for weight loss videos would be high. There are a lot of YouTube superstars that are making good income, but I think that's very challenging. I've been able to monetize my audience by taking them to my blog where I have great products and services. I also make money recommending other people's products, as an affiliate. For example, if I do a YouTube video that shares my results of using the Vitamix blender that costs $500, and people see my review and use my link to buy the blender, I'll be making more money as an affiliate as compared to the ad revenue I'll make from that video. Nonetheless, if you're doing very funny and entertaining videos that become viral on YouTube, you are going to get a lot of ad revenue.

Me: I check your monthly goal report regularly and I can see tremendous progress in your income levels in the last year. Which aspect of your business was the prime contributor for this success?

Stefan: Until 2013, I was putting out a lot of content, but I didn't really have anything to sell. When I launched my K Money Mastery course, many of my YouTube followers who loved what I was doing, bought it. So, one of the keys was creating my own products. Another thing happened in 2014. I was doing fairly well. I was making around $20,000 per month. I then decided to upgrade my lifestyle. I moved to a penthouse in Vancouver on the 48th floor of Sheraton Wall Center. I bought a sports car as well. All of a sudden, I had way more credibility behind what I was saying. People were able to see the before and after. More people started buying my course and more people wanted coaching from me. I know it sounds a bit weird and shallow, but it was an interesting lesson for me. From February 2014, I started sharing my monthly goals and progress which I think gave more credibility to what I was doing.

Me: By openly sharing your goals report, don't you feel accountable for everything in your life? Doesn't it scare you?

Stefan: Not really. It creates a lot of pressure, but I think that's a good thing because pressure creates diamonds. When you put that kind of demand on yourself, that kind of pressure, you're more likely to show up, you're more likely to make it happen. If I have a bad month, it's okay because my transparency in showing failure makes more people relate to me. If you go through challenges or failure and overcome it, you become even more inspirational to even more people.

4. Kindle Publishing

If you have a message in you, a story to share or an experience to write about, you need not go looking for a big traditional publisher anymore. Amazon's Kindle platform has made it very easy for authors to self-publish their work and reach out to millions of readers across the world. Steve Scott has been able to build a thriving business by just writing books on topics close to his heart. Read on to find out how you can do it too.

Interview with Steve Scott
(http://stevescottsite.com)

Me: *How did you decide that Habit is the niche that you need to focus on?*

Steve: When you work from home, when you run your own business you really need to be very structured. As a by-product of running internet businesses, I got pretty good at routines, schedules and habits. I've always been into running and exercising on a daily basis. I guess I got a bit tired of writing just about internet businesses, though even now I do enjoy it. Some people were writing to me saying that I am making money by writing about how to make money. They said it's easy to do what I was saying in the internet business, but I can't replicate this in another market. I took that as a personal challenge. I wanted to prove that I could do this in a market that has nothing to do with making money. I didn't think it would take off the way it did.

Me: What amazes me is that most authors write one or two books in a lifetime. But, you've written more than 40 books in two years. How do you do that?

Steve: I would say that it goes back to habits and routines. I have a timeline for every book. Every time I start a new book I print out a checklist sheet and go through it. It's just the matter of sitting down and writing. I try to carve out the first part of the morning and part of the afternoon for writing. I follow the Pomodoro technique where I do 25 minutes on, 5 minutes off. I used to keep track of my daily word counts. I used to track where I was and how many words I wrote to give a better understanding of where I worked best. I realized that early afternoon was my optimum writing time at Starbucks. Understanding your own natural rhythms and scheduling time for those specific moments of the day helps.

Me: So writing at 5 am need not be the best time for everybody, right?

Steve: I would say that the morning routine is good for people who can't find time during the day, so that they don't find excuses for not writing. But, I know people that write very well at night. At the end of the day, you should do what works best for you.

Me: When I ask my friends to write books, most of them are skeptical because they feel a book has to be 200-300 pages long. In your opinion, what's the optimum length of a Kindle book?

Steve: I actually did an analysis of all my books and the one that has consistently sold the best was 14,000 words long. The 30,000-35,000 words books don't sell consistently well. I would say that anywhere between 15,000-20,000 words would be a good length. That could be between 90 and 120 pages on Kindle.

Me: *Have you started experimenting with the traditional offline book stores?*

Steve: I have 100% invested in Amazon. Down the road, Amazon will not be the only game in town. For now, I am building as big an audience as possible on Amazon. In a couple of months, I am planning to move two books out of Amazon and start testing the other platforms. As far as physical book stores are concerned, I think it's an 80-20 rule. It looks like a lot of effort for what may not be a huge return. So, that's low on my priority list.

Me: *You try a lot of marketing strategies like emailers, Slideshare, Facebook marketing etc. Which one gives you the maximum returns for your investment and time?*

Steve: Without a doubt - email marketing. Through Facebook ads I'm trying to target people who have read my Kindle book, but haven't signed up to my email list. But my #1 long term strategy is email marketing. Probably why I'm doing well is because I realized from the very beginning that email marketing could really help drive sales on Amazon.

Me: *You've started co-authoring books with Rebecca Livermore. Tell us a little about that.*

Steve: It helps me save some time in the book production process and also have someone add their own experiences into it. I thought it was worth testing. I have some book ideas that I want to have it my way and not have someone else's input. I think in the long term, a combination of working with a partner and working on your own would be good. You can work with a partner, if you ever come across a person who can really add value to a book or has a unique perspective or has a specialized skill that you don't have.

Me: When your "Habit Stacking" book was launched you made more than $60,000 in that month. But the income dropped to $30-40k in a couple of months. How do you deal with these ups and downs in business?

Steve: It's hard. But I tend not to have an expensive taste. I try to keep the quality of my life pretty low. So during the dips I can afford to live on less than $7-8k. I put this money in savings or investing in future business. But mentally, it's not easy. When you have a successful month, don't go out and buy a fancy car or get a million dollar mortgage on a house, because this money could go away at any given point. Plan for the rainy day. I did take a vacation to Italy during summer which cost me a lot of money. But beyond that I drive the same Honda Civic and live in the same apartment!

Me: When you were working on your latest book "The Exercise Habit" you sent a mail to all your readers asking for their #1 challenge in developing the exercise habit. That's a very intelligent way of involving the readers into the content of the book. How has this strategy worked?

Steve: It was an amazing experience. I printed out a stack of every single email I got and went through it. It helped me to structure the framework of the book and helped me realize what people are going through after reading pages and pages of their challenges. Moving forward, I am going to pull my audience and ask them questions before I start writing any book.

Me: If you were to start your Kindle publishing business today, would you do anything differently?

Steve: I would do certain things the same way like picking a niche, email list and having a blog. But I would add one thing to it. I would choose a niche where I can easily find the market through

Facebook ads, blogs. The problem with the Habit niche is that it's very hard to target that audience because everyone wants to build different habits. There's no customer avatar. Another piece of advice would be to look for products that you can sell in the backend like affiliate products. This would help you to scale up your business, without having to depend on Amazon.

Me: People hardly get to see you in front of the camera. Why are you avoiding video as a medium?

Steve: I can definitely do video marketing in the form of screenshots! My upcoming self- publishing course primarily has video content, though I am not very comfortable with the medium. It's been a challenge for me to face a video screen but I want to improve upon that skill. I would like to focus on what's working for me rightly now rather than doing everything all at once. For me Kindle is making me money right now. So I don't want to lose out on something that's growing by focusing on too many platforms.

Me: So, one need not have their presence in all the platforms, right?

Steve: Yes, not necessary. And I would say don't delay on building your email list, no matter which platform you choose.

5. Amazon physical products

You can partner with the world's largest e-commerce store to build a business from home. You can earn thousands of dollars every month by being the bridge between manufacturers and Amazon. In the below interview, Andy Dew talks about how he is able to travel the world after setting up a business that almost runs on auto-pilot.

Interview with Andy Dew
(www.itsdewable.com)

Me: Since when did you start selling products on Amazon?

Andy: It was a little over four years ago. I had some previous experience running an eBay drop-shipping business when I was in high school. Then a few years later, I started selling video games that I bought at great deals from retail stores on Amazon. At that time, I didn't know about Fulfillment by Amazon. I was just selling out of my basement, shipping every item individually to customers.

Me: *So, you had to maintain the inventory yourself?*

Andy: Yes! I had to take twenty video games to the post office, and individually package each one, write down the customers' addresses, and I was making just six to seven dollars for every sale which became a huge pain after a point. And then eventually, I found out about FBA - Fulfillment by Amazon, and then I was able to ship my entire inventory to Amazon in one shipment with discounted UPS shipping, and then when it's sold, they took care of the rest. They also took care of the customer service, so for me, it was like a match made in heaven!

Me: *So, Fulfillment by Amazon (FBA) is actually a service that Amazon offers, right?*

Andy: Yes! Amazon saw the need to take over the least enjoyable part of being a merchant. Instead of waiting for the video games to sell and ship them to customers individually, I was able to take all those games and just go drop it off at any UPS store, and then they got it sent to Amazon. Then when the products get listed on Amazon and it starts selling, Amazon would ship out the product from their warehouse to the customer. If a customer has any complaints or concerns, they deal directly with Amazon, and it's covered under the Amazon return policy and exchange policy. Amazon prime members favor the items that you are selling because when the product is fulfilled by Amazon, it qualifies for free supersaver shipping. It gives you quite an advantage because your brand comes off as a little bit more professional because it is coming in an Amazon box as opposed to an ordinary box.

Me: Don't you need to have your own brand to sell on Amazon?

Andy: Not necessary. You can source products from retail shops, other online retailers or directly from the manufacturers and sell them on Amazon. You can also private label these products to create your own brand. But only if your product is unique and original, it's worth the effort to brand your products. Most Amazon customers don't even know that they are buying from a third party seller. So it doesn't require you to have your own branding.

Me: *Do you have to be living in the United States to do this or you could just be anywhere?*

Andy: You can be anywhere! I have a really good friend of mine who is a very successful Amazon seller, and he is from Jamaica. He successfully sells on Amazon.com and now he expanded his business to sell on Amazon.co.uk and Amazon.de as well.

Me: *What's the real potential of selling physical products on Amazon? I've heard about people who are making $50,000 to $100,000 per month. Is it really the money that they make or are they just bluffing?*

Andy: Yes, these numbers are possible. But a lot of Amazon sellers will talk about their total revenue and that is the amount of sales before Amazon has taken their fee and without accounting for the inventory cost. I had a month where my revenue was like upwards of $80,000, but my profits were less than $30,000. As a general rule of thumb, you usually take home 28-35%, depending on the type of items that you're sourcing. Amazon takes a good chunk but they also do a good amount of work for you!

Me: You were mentioning toys and games as one of the categories you are into, so how does one decide the right product for them when they're first entering into the Amazon market?

Andy: I look at two things. First, I see the demand for a product on Amazon, which can be determined by checking the Amazon bestseller rank. If a similar product on Amazon has a good ranking, the chance of my product selling well is pretty high. I then see the number of sellers competing for that product because something might be in demand but if you're competing with ninety other sellers, you know that's a lot of competition there. I would also ensure that everything that I bought was good in price difference. I usually buy things at 50% of the selling price. Sometimes I would even buy something for $10 sell it for $35.

Me: So once you decide on the product, where do you source them from? Across the world or only from the United States?

Andy: It's a mixture. More recently, I've been sourcing from China but I like sourcing from retail stores as well. The way that I started doing it was I would actually go into physical stores and I would scan the barcodes of products using an app on my Smartphone. That would bring up the sales rank data and if I enter my buyer cost, it would run the calculations for me and show me what my net profit would be. This is a great way to find the price discrepancies and the demand and then you meet that demand by carrying that product.

Me: *When you are sourcing from places like China, do you still get to see the product, or does the manufacturer take care of everything?*

Andy: You can teach manufacturers how to send products directly to Amazon, if they're open to it. The only tricky thing is they would have access to your account to some degree unless you printed the shipment label yourself and emailed it to them.

Me: *How much does a person starting off should invest into this business?*

Andy: Typically, I tell people to start up with at least $500 to start buying some of your first inventory. If you are sourcing from other retail sites, you can get their free shipping deals. If you are sourcing from a store, you should be able to use a coupon or their rewards program to save some money. If you want to go into more bulk orders, it's good to place a first order of around $1000. One thing you should make sure is the quality of the items, especially if you're getting them from China. I've had plenty of experiences where I order too many and when they arrive, they are not up to the standard.

Me: On your website www.itsdewable.com, you have some online courses on selling on Amazon. Can you tell us a little bit about that?

Andy: That site is great for beginners because you get a really thorough step by step process of the basics of selling on Amazon. The model I teach specifically is how to source retail products online, and even though I did start to source in the physical stores, my goal in creating Dewable was to be the first course that showed people how to use this model and take it totally online and then totally automate it.

Me: *You are actually living the model that you're preaching. Right now you live in Thailand, so you are able to work from anywhere in the world, right?*

Andy: Yes! I am in Chiang Mai, Thailand now. In the first year of my marriage, my wife and I traveled to ten different countries.

6. Udemy courses

Are you passionate about teaching? Then this one is for you! People now prefer learning through online courses rather than going to college as it saves them a lot of time and money. You can take advantage of this trend my creating online courses on subjects of your expertise and selling them through Udemy.com. Discover the tools and strategies that Rob Cubbon has used to build a successful business on Udemy.

Interview with Rob Cubbon
(www.robcubbon.com)

Me: Way back in 2006, you made that bold decision of quitting your job, right?

Rob: Well I didn't really make a bold decision ever actually! In 2005, I launched robcubbon.com, but it was nothing - as it was just a static html website. At the time I was freelancing and getting paid by the hour to do graphic design work, and then I started blogging in 2006 after installing Wordpress and I started getting work from the blog. I got work to do at home, which was kind of like my business. But, it took me two years to give up the freelance work, because it obviously didn't happen overnight.

Me: There's actually quite a lot of difference between a freelancer and an entrepreneur. Generating passive income is totally different from working by the hour, right?

Rob: Yes, I don't know what the definition of the word entrepreneur is. I think you can call yourself an entrepreneur if you work for yourself. When I started off on my own, I was still getting paid by the hour, but I saw myself as a business rather than a person who was freelancing. I was responsible for everything - the money, getting the work, the client, doing the work, getting paid, etc. Passive income comes at a different stage.

Me: Right, so unless you go through this process, you wouldn't have reached where you are right now.

Rob: Exactly I think the freelance work really helped me because it's easier to get money as a freelancer when you're starting out on your own, than make passive income.

Me: *So which was the real passive income business you actually started, was it Udemy first?*

Rob: No, actually, first I sold PDF reports on my website. Then I guess Udemy was the biggest and the most important platform for me as that's where I took off. I was making money before then, but Udemy really took it to the next level.

Me: *I think Udemy is a wonderful platform because you can take whatever you know in whichever area, and you can convert it into a course, and sell it online and people from across the world can be your students, right?*

Rob: Yeah, definitely! In fact, all my business, be it web designing, Udemy course or Kindle books are location independent, so that's how I am able to live in Thailand.

Me: *You have twelve courses on Udemy. What kind of research do you do before starting a course? How do you find out whether there is a market for it or not?*

Rob: I was blogging and was on YouTube for a long time and I was creating free content. This gave me market research data. If you are blogging, you have Google Analytics to show you what's popular, and if you're on YouTube, then you've got your video views to show you what's popular. And that really educated me on what was going to be a very good course. People would also email me asking for more information on certain topics like how to create a website that looks exactly like how you want it to or how to run a web designing business. So, I was sure these topics would work well for my Udemy courses.

Me: I think irrespective of what platform you choose online, whether it's Udemy or YouTube, it's important to have a blog, so that you can directly connect with your target market and get free feedback from them.

Rob: Absolutely yes, you just get great information through blog comments and emails. You can also start collecting email addresses of your potential customers, and that's another great source of information. Then you can email them and ask what they want to know more about and you'll get hundreds of replies!

Me: You are not just dependant on Udemy, but you also have your membership site. So why would someone choose your membership site over the Udemy course and which is more profitable or better as a long-term proposition for you?

Rob: People get more personal overseeing from me on my site because there are 300 people on my site, and I have over 50,000 students on Udemy! I started with Udemy over two years ago and I've just started selling courses on my own site. Definitely the most profitable one is Udemy. But, what if something happens to Udemy? Competition could increase there or I could lose the students overnight! It's not a good idea to put all your eggs in one basket.

Me: Very true! So what do you think is the bare minimum requirement in terms of investment to create a Udemy course?

Rob: It doesn't take much of financial and time investment. You could get away with just Screen Flow for Mac or Camtasia for PC for doing screen capture videos and a decent microphone that costs $15-100 (I've got the Samsung Meteor). I would advise you to do a little bit more than just screen casting and your voice. It would be nice to show your face just a little at the beginning and at the end of videos.

Me: *Yeah, so that students know there is a real person behind the course.*

Rob: Yes. You can do that on your smart phone or you can buy a cheap HD video camera as well. You don't need DSLRs. You will make mistakes while recording. Your first few videos won't be as good as the next few videos, but it's important to get started. You should definitely start with Udemy because it's the biggest one. But if you see a bit of success on Udemy, you should really go and upload your courses to Skill Feed and Skill Share almost straight away.

Me: *Sure, the more platforms, the more exposure. Can you share with us the three things that you are doing differently from other Udemy instructors that are helping you get you huge traffic in terms of students signing up?*

Rob: There are a few things that definitely work for me. First of all, I had the blog and the readership which gave me the email list. I had enough people who were interested in what I was doing and they would follow me to Udemy and buy my courses.

Once you get a bit of success, Udemy themselves will promote your courses in their internal way. They'll only do that if people buy your courses and give a good feedback. The second thing I did was to create some free courses early on. This helped me gather lots of students who later upgraded to my paid courses. The third thing is to have multiple courses. This helps me to cross promote my courses to my students.

Me: If you were to start off with Udemy today, would you do anything differently?

Rob: My earlier courses were horrible! So if I were to start today, I would buy a better microphone and invest in a software like ScreenFlow or Camtasia. I'd ask more questions to my audience. I'd make shorter courses with shorter lectures. Five minute long lectures are okay. I used to make fifteen minute long lectures that would send everyone to sleep!

7. Mobile Apps

Just check how many mobile apps you are using on your smart phone. You can take any niche of your choice and create a useful mobile app for your target market. List them on the Apple or Android app store and see your business grow with every download you get. Let's hear Alex Genedinik's story of how he became the guru of business apps.

Interview with Alex Genadinik
(www.problemio.com)

Me: So when you started out into the mobile apps business, did you start with the mindset that this is what you want to focus on or you just wanted to try out this business opportunity and see whether it will do well?

Alex: I was a web developer and this apps thing was happening and everybody was just talking about apps. As a developer you have to always keep learning, otherwise you become obsolete. So for me I just had to make it to learn it.

Me: *So, was that the next logical step for you from a web developer to an app developer?*

Alex: Yes! I like building consumer products that are easy to go to market with and compared to big data products, apps are much easier, and much more fun and interesting. I didn't think it was going to be big. I just wanted to put something in my resume. So apps are a logical choice. I had a website at that time which wasn't doing well. I had the intention of having entrepreneurs come in and discuss their business ideas. But they didn't want to do that on the web for some reasons, because they wanted privacy. So, I built my first app for them, just like a toy app.

Me: *So you didn't do any kind of a marketing search or surveys before getting into the business app?*

Alex: Nothing, it was just for me to learn. The first time I launched it on Android, it didn't even have a logo. It was the worst app in Android market, but I noticed that it started getting one or two downloads a day which was very exciting.

Me: *Did you initially launch a free app?*

Alex: Yeah, it was a free app. Every day I would learn something new and I'd put it into the app and I'd re-launch the app. The cool thing about Android is that you get to update it as much as you want, unlike Apple where you have to wait a week for their review team to get back. Pretty quickly I ran out of things to build, so I added this really simple feature after which everything took off and that feature was for people to ask me any questions related to business. And every time they ask me a question, I realized I should add that feature to the app. More questions, more app features. And pretty soon I ended up building exactly what they were telling me that they needed.

Me: So you were getting the idea directly from the customers?

Alex: Yes, directly from them. In a matter of one and a half months my app became number one for the word business plan on Android, it was the highest rated business app on Android, it was at 4.8 out of 5 stars for a long time. I then made an Apple app for that. I then realized that people were always having four major issues: finding business ideas, business planning, raising money and marketing their business.

Me: That's like a step-by-step process that any entrepreneur has to anyway go through, right?

Alex: Yeah exactly. So I built it into a four apps series. To have it all in one app was going to make it very bulky. So I had a business idea app, business plan app, fund raising app and marketing app. Very soon for the keyword "business" on the Android store, my apps were in the number 1, 3, 5 and 8 positions. I had four on the top 10. I think I'm close to a million downloads now.

Me: Wow, that's awesome! Alex, you have a strong technical background, so creating mobile apps was a natural progression for you. Is this a good side business for people without technical knowledge? Is it enough to just have the idea and outsource the app creation to a developer?

Alex: My number one suggestion would be to learn how to make it on your own. But, no one takes that advice. Usually what they do is that they hire an agency or a freelance developer because it's just faster to go to market. But when your hire someone, it's a lot of money because you have to constantly keep upgrading your app in the competitive market place.

Me: How long will it take or how difficult is it to launch mobile apps on your own?

Alex: If you do it the right way by taking an online course and using the right resources, you can have a basic app within one or two months. As you progress, you can improve the design or add more features, to make it a fully functional app.

Me: The reason why many people don't become entrepreneurs is because they don't want to launch something that's not perfect.

Alex: Many industries are very forgiving. If you get very bad reviews, you can pull down that app, improve it and then re-launch it. I think there's value in getting in the game. I now have a big YouTube presence. People keep telling me that the sound quality has to improve and they make fun of my background. So, I always try to get better and better because now the competition online is so fierce.

Me: *When the competition is so fierce, how does one choose the right niche to enter?*

Alex: There is a blog post called "Most Startups should be Deer Hunters" by the famous investor Mark Suster. He says, if you are hunting, you don't want to hunt rabbits because there's not enough meat, you don't want to hunt elephants because you'll never kill one, but you want to find something just right in the middle like a deer. You can do this by searching for apps in the app store.

Me: *So, you would search for some potential keywords and see the kind of other apps that are already in the market and then you'll see the kind of downloads they get to understand the profitability in that niche and then decide to go into it, right?*

Alex: Yeah, absolutely!

Me: *You have hundreds of videos on your YouTube channel. Does that help you to market your apps?*

Alex: Though I have around 400,000 views on my YouTube channel, 98% of my app downloads come from internal app store search. People who like to consume videos do not necessarily like to read books or use apps. So cross platform marketing is difficult. What I find easier is to have a catalogue of products. So, on the app stores I have a catalogue of apps, on Kindle I have a catalogue of books, on Udemy I have a catalog of courses.

Me: Yes! You have 43 courses on Udemy and 20,000 students! How did you manage that?

Alex: I initially made a lot of business related courses myself. I then ran out of topics to teach really quickly. So now, I partner with people who are experts. So, I am more like a director.

Me: That's amazing! If you were to start your online businesses from scratch, would you do anything differently?

Alex: Yes. I would get mentors. Or in the least, I advise people to get some educational materials like taking online courses, because it's a cheaper way to get coaching.

My Top 10 Takeaways From The Interviews

1. Choose any platform, but make sure you are passionate about the niche or product you choose.

2. It's important to have your own website or blog. Even if you predominantly use other sites like Amazon or Udemy to sell, have a way to bring people to your own website.

3. Create a great opt-in offer on your website to build an email list of followers.

4. You may monetize your blog or podcast using ads or affiliate links, but creating your own products should be your long-term strategy.

5. Don't wait for your product or service to become perfect. Just launch them. You can always improve them as you progress.

6. Offer great value for free upfront. This will help you build the trust and relationship with your followers.

7. It's important to have a catalog of products to encourage repeat customers.

8. If you are not the expert, you can still have a successful online business by collaborating with experts.

9. Define your ideal customer avatar in detail at the very beginning itself. This will help you get clarity about what your target customers want and how to reach them.

10. Start with one platform. Grow it and then start having your presence on other platforms as well.

Action Steps

1. Browse through the websites of all the seven online entrepreneurs featured here. Do some research on their content and their products.

2. Decide on the platform that you think you would be most comfortable in.

Step 6

———————~———————

Learn, Research and Study

"To double your income, triple your rate of learning."
– Robin Sharma

All of us want our current year to be better than our previous year. Einstein said that the definition of insanity is doing the same thing over and over again and expecting different results. We therefore need to become better in terms of our knowledge, habits, health, productivity, goals etc., so that we can achieve more than the previous year. The only way to do this is by constantly learning and upgrading ourselves. I am a strong believer of life-long learning. Education doesn't stop with college. Learning the tricks of the trade is all the more important when you are transforming from an employee to an entrepreneur.

Here are some of the proven ways to learn a new skill:

Read a book on your chosen side business

By reading a book we literally get into the mind of another person. I may have to spend a $1000 per hour to get personal coaching from an expert. But I'll just have to spend $3 to read a book written by the expert. Read at least three good books written by the top leaders in your chosen online platform. This will put you in the right frame of mind and also offer you the basic knowledge that you need to start your side hustle.

Follow blogs

There is so much happening in the blogging world. People share their experiences, learning and discoveries on a daily basis. Look out for the blogs of people who are authorities in your industry and subscribe to their blogs and podcasts. Also, follow a couple of people who are a year or two ahead of you. You'll be able to relate to them better as they've ventured on this journey just a few years before you. The online business is an ever evolving one. Blogs help you keep abreast with the latest developments, which you may not find in books written a year back. Having said that, I would advise you not to follow tons of gurus. You will not just get overwhelmed by information overload, but you'll also end up wasting too much time on the internet.

Watch how-to videos on YouTube

For me, YouTube is like going to university on a scholarship! There is so much high quality free content out there that you can literally learn how to do anything. If you are planning to create a mobile app, you can find videos on how to do that. If you want to start your blog, there are videos to teach you how to set up a WordPress website in 15 minutes. You can also subscribe to a few YouTube channels that regularly post videos related to your niche.

Take a course on the subject

Joining a specialized course in your niche or your chosen online platform will help you dive deep into the subject. This is important, especially when you are starting out. It's very helpful to be taken through the step-by-step process by a person who has already achieved what you want to achieve. Most of us need this extra push to start. A good course is going to cost you money. This will give you all the more reasons to start your business and get the returns on your investment. Udemy is a good place to look for an online course. Warrior Forum also offers good advice from other internet marketers about which course to choose.

Go to seminars

Though self-learning through books, blogs and videos can help you to a great extend, live training in seminars can take you to a different level altogether. Something magical happens when you learn from a mentor with a live audience. The positive energy in the room will drive you to take massive action. Seminars are also great places to meet and network with like-minded people. You may connect with some people after the seminar and continue learning from each other's progress. You may also end up doing business with some of them later! Since I became an entrepreneur I've been attending seminars once every three months. I guarantee you that the return on this investment will be 10x.

Join a mastermind

A mastermind is a group of individuals who meet regularly (typically once a week or twice a month) to discuss each other's goals and progress. They also offer advice and feedback to one another to grow their businesses. The members of a mastermind usually have a common interest. You can look for active mastermind groups in your area by checking meetup.com. Or you can create one yourself by inviting 4-8 people whom you think will benefit from each other. This works brilliantly if members are committed and have the mindset to contribute. The more you give, the more you get. These days, online masterminds have become popular where people living in different parts of the world come together over a weekly Skype call and exchange notes on each other's progress. This sense of community motivates members to take action and stand up for each other's goals.

Find an accountability partner

If you join a mastermind, you can choose one of its members as your accountability partner. If you are finding it hard to find or organize a mastermind, at least do yourself the favor of finding one person whom you can trust and make that person your accountability partner. We as human beings are fundamentally lazy. Most of us need a whacking on our back to wake up and take action. We need someone who will hold us accountable for doing what we are supposed to do. Your accountability partner will do just that! He/she need not have any idea about your industry or niche. He/she should just practice tough love by genuinely caring about your success and committing to accountability calls. You should list down your daily/weekly/monthly goals and share it with each other. You can get on a call every day or every week and monitor your partner's progress. My life changed after I found my accountability partner while doing an online course. Stephen lives in New Zealand and calls me every Monday. If not for him, I would not have started writing regularly to publish this book within a month.

Hire a coach

Lady Gaga has a vocal coach. Roger Federer has a tennis coach. Every successful person works with a coach. You may not think it's important to have a coach when you are starting out in a new profession. But, if you want to excel in it, you'll most definitely need a coach. Most online marketers have a well-formatted coaching program which you can enroll in. You can contact a person who has already achieved what you want to achieve and who has the experience of mentoring many students. This will shorten your learning curve as your coach will hold you accountable, direct you to the best resources, warn you from potential mistakes and motivate you to chase your dreams.

Investing in the stock market or real estate may be risky, but investing in yourself will always fetch you huge returns. Learning will always give you an edge over the other players in your business. It will also give you the confidence you'll need to start your business, which will eventually help you quit your job and enjoy your freedom.

Action Steps

1. Do check out the Resources section at the end of the book for some useful courses, books, blogs and experts in the online marketing business. Make an immediate start by buying at least one book, following one blog and subscribing to one YouTube channel.

2. Do intensive research on people who have established their online presence in your niche.

For example, if you want to start a marriage advice business, look for all the relationship coaches who have an online business. Study their content and method of delivery and look for ways in which you can be different and offer something better.

3. Based on your learning, create a blueprint to start and run an online business in you chosen niche. Write down all the steps involved in starting your side business.

Step 7

---~---

Start The Business, Grow It & Quit Your Job!

"Done is better than perfect."
- Sheryl Sandberg

After laying a strong foundation in your chosen line of business in Step 6, it's now time to put your learning into practice. The money will start coming in only after you start taking action. If you have chosen your niche, say vegan cooking, have decided your ideal online platform, say publishing a cookbook series on Kindle, and have read a few books on how to publish on Kindle or have signed up for a course on the subject, you are good to go.

Do not wait to become an expert in that industry before you start your side business. By coming so far you are already ahead of most people. Also, your target market is not everyone. Your business is going to cater to the people who are one or more steps behind you in your field of interest. Don't compare yourself with the celebrity chefs who get featured in magazines and TV. You'll get there sooner or later if you keep taking action on a regular, consistent basis.

Brand your business

Give your business a unique and interesting name. By doing this right at the beginning, it will start feeling more real. Also, spend some dollars to create a logo, business cards and stationery. You can get all this done for $20 on fiverr.com. Most people will find this unnecessary when they are starting out, but in my opinion a business takes shape only when you can physically see it in the form of the logo.

Also, block a domain name on godaddy.com as soon as you decide on the name. You'll need this for sure when you are in the online space.

Set targets for the business

It is always more powerful if you start with the end in mind. As your primary objective is to quit your job, your key focus should be to grow your business to make more money than your day job salary. Your target should also be time-bound. If you make $5,000 per month in your job, your target for the business should be to generate $5,000 in monthly profit within the next six months. Also, set yourself monthly business targets that increase progressively so that you don't aim for the sky in the very first month. Connect with other people who are in the similar line of business and get a rough idea about the numbers they are reaching. This will help you set realistic targets for yourself.

Set up a home office

Even though you'll be working on your side business from home, before or after your day job, you'll need to set aside a dedicated work space at home. Don't work on your couch one day, at the dinner table the other day and on the bed the third day. If you assign a specific zone at home for work, it'll help you get into the right mindset to work and improve your productivity drastically. You need not set up anything fancy; a corner table that's big enough to accommodate your laptop will do. Let your family know about this arrangement so that they won't disturb you when you are in your home office area.

Plan your day

You can efficiently make use of your 24 hours only if you have a plan. The first few months of your side business could be quite challenging until the time you leave your full-time job as you need to strike a balance between the two. If you are going to be at your office for eight hours a day, then you can realistically set aside just two hours for your side-hustle, which is good enough. The quality of work you accomplish in these two hours is more important than the quantity of time you spend.

The best way to plan your day is to reverse engineer it from the goals you have set for your side business. For example, if you want to make $5,000 from your online business by the 6th month, you should chalk out a detailed plan to accomplish this. You can get some clues from the people you are following online in your niche or the courses you are taking.

Once you have a six month plan in place, break it down into monthly goals. Write down the action steps to achieve the monthly goals. Break the first month's action plan into weekly list of things to do.

From your weekly plan, arrive at your daily plan. I typically plan my week on Sunday night and plan my day on the night before. This habit will give you a laser sharp focus on you business and will help you achieve your goals faster.

Ensure that these two hours of business work doesn't clash with your family time. Make extra time for yourself by waking up an hour early and going to bed an hour late.

Generate more passive income than your salary

If you consistently provide great value by creating ebooks, videos, blog posts, podcasts, videos or any other content or product in you niche, you are bound to get a great following of happy customers online. But this doesn't happen overnight. It takes perseverance and hard work to reach a level where your income from your online business will exceed the monthly salary you get from your employer.

The beauty of the internet is that you don't have to wait a lifetime to see this happen. It can happen in a few months' time if you take consistent action every day. It took me three months to go from $0 to $1,000 in my Kindle publishing business. But to move from $1,000 to $4,000, it took me just another three months! That's the compounding effect you'll see once you master the skills and start getting loyal followers. Stay calm and keep hustling. It's only a matter of time before the income from your online business exceeds your salary!

Send your resignation letter to your boss!

This is the day most people have been waiting for. I would suggest you to draft your resignation letter the day you start your side business. This will act as a reminder and motivate you to keep working on your business. The day you feel that your passive income has become consistent and you have saved a bit to cover your expenses for the next few months, you know you are ready to take the leap.

With lots of gratitude for your boss and your company, send them your resignation letter. Help them in every way you can for a smooth transition so that you leave them on a good note. This is important because you want to start your journey as a full-time entrepreneur with a lot of positivity!

What Next?

If you have followed all the seven steps in the book, you will have quit your job by now or at least making progress in the journey towards freedom. Congratulations!

Set up systems and structures

Now that you are an entrepreneur, you need to have systems and structures to run your company.

Hire a certified accountant or take legal advice to register your company so that you can enjoy tax benefits based on the prevailing tax laws in your country. Create a bank account in your company's name and start tracking all the income and expenses on a regular basis.

Have a process to create reports to monitor the business numbers. This will help you track your performance over time and help you take informed decisions in future. Track everything that you can possibly track. Visitors to your website, clicks on different pages, number of opt-ins, sales during promotions, performance of ads, email open rate, etc. Only the things that get measured can be improved.

Create a schedule for every activity in your business and stick to it. For example, writing blogs, shooting videos, managing Facebook page, launching new products, conducting webinars, etc. Planning will improve your productivity which will in turn increase your profits.

Build a team of virtual assistants

If you've been doing most of the activities in your business yourself, it's time to outsource some of them to virtual assistants. You can hire a few permanent VAs who can perform all the routine and repetitive tasks in your business. You can hire specialists like developers, designers, editors, etc. to work on specific projects.

Once you find a few good people you can start managing their work using project management apps from anywhere in the world. It is also wise to create some VA training videos so that every time you hire a new VA, you can just make that person go through these how-to videos instead of spending your time training that person. Continue doing the core activities in the business that cannot be done by anyone else.

Go on a mini-vacation

After all the hard work you've done, you truly deserve a vacation. Once you have a couple of virtual assistants who can manage the show while you are gone, it's time to travel with your friends and family to a destination that'll help you unwind and rejuvenate. Most successful entrepreneurs make it a practice to holiday once every three months. This may look like a bit too much. But one week of relaxation can prepare your mind for the next three months of focused work.

Extend your online presence

Over time, if you consistently work on improving your online business, you will gain mastery over it. Once you start generating a steady flow of income from one online platform, start preparing yourself to venture into another platform. Remember to go back to Step 5 to choose the next platform and Step 6 to learn the tools of the trade so that you can make the best use of the new platform to reach out to more potential customers and grow your following. This also helps you in diversifying your online portfolio.

Conclusion

⌁

Thank you so much for choosing to read my book and taking the initiative to read until the end. I highly appreciate your commitment to improve the quality of your life. If you are working as an employee, I am sure this book will have opened the doors to the wide variety of opportunities available if you choose to become an entrepreneur. If you are self-employed or own a business, I hope you will have discovered new ways to take your business online and earn passive income. If you are a student, stay-at-home-mom, retired person or unemployed, the book will have helped you in utilizing your unique talents to help the world and make some money as a by-product.

In the last few years, the internet has changed the way the world works. Anyone who sincerely pursues an online business has the potential to make a fortune. I will consider this book to be a success if you follow the action steps in this book and start your own online business. If you are able to quit your job eventually, I will be even more thrilled!

If you have enjoyed reading the book, I request you kindly **write your review on Amazon** by clicking HERE! Your feedback is very important as it will help me continue to write books that add value to your life.

Sharing is caring! Do share this book link with your friends and family by clicking the buttons below. You can have a profound impact on someone's life by showing them a way to follow their passion and start a business.

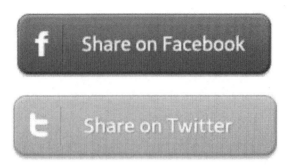

Also, make sure you join our **private Facebook group** of Job Escape Planners, where you can meet like-minded people and discuss your online business ideas and job escape strategies directly with me. Here's the link to the FB group:

https://www.facebook.com/groups/jobescapeplanners/

I wish you lots of success in your new journey. I am eagerly waiting to hear your success story! Thank you!

Free Bonus #1

As a token of thanks for downloading my book, I would like to give you 100% FREE access to watch the uncut videos of the interviews I did with 7 successful online entrepreneurs - Andy Dew, Alex Genadinik, John Lee Dumas, Nick Loper, Rob Cubbon, Stefan Pylarinos and Steve Scott!

CLICK HERE TO ACCESS

Or go to

http://jyotsnaramachandran.com/freebonus

Free Bonus #2

~

If you are too busy to read this book completely, you can't give that excuse anymore! I'm going to give you free access to download the audio book of Job Escape Plan! You can now listen to it while driving or running!

CLICK HERE TO ACCESS

Or go to

http://jyotsnaramachandran.com/freebonus

You can also listen to this audio book for FREE on **Amazon's Audible** and start your FREE 30-day Trial of this audio book membership site.

Audio book on Amazon:

http://www.amazon.com/Job-Escape-Plan-Business-Freedom/dp/B0100NYCIM/

Audio book on Audible:

http://www.audible.com/pd/Business/Job-Escape-Plan-Audiobook/B00ZROOLWW

Resources

Books

Four Hour Work Week by Timothy Ferriss

Crush It by Gary Vaynerchuk

Book Launch by Chandler Bolt and James Roper

Kindle Publishing Package by Steve Scott

Podcast Launch by John Lee Dumas

Virtual Assistant Assistant by Nick Loper

Create the Website You Want by Rob Cubbon

Online Courses

Podcaster's Paradise by John Lee Dumas

KMoney Mastery by Stefan Pylarinos

Kindle Launch Plan by Nick Loper

Amazon Selling Course by Andy Dew

Mobile Apps course by Alex Genadinik

Udemy Passive Income by Harshajyoti Das

Passive Income course by Rob Cubbon

Blogs

Smart Passive Income

Become a Blogger

Project Life Mastery

Pro Blogger

Side Hustle Nation

Entrepreneur on Fire

Jyotsna Ramachandran (Yes, that's my blog!)

Domain Name

GoDaddy

I've tried a couple of other domain name sites, but I keep going back to GoDaddy because it is easy to use, pricing is competitive and their billing is transparent.

Website Hosting

BlueHost

I've tried Hostgator, Big Rock and BlueHost. BlueHost wins hands down because of its customer service!

Website Platform

WordPress

This is the only web design platform I've tried. It is super easy to use and is perfect for non-techies like me. 😊

Website Template

ThemeForest

You can choose from among the thousands of beautiful and functional WordPress templates available on ThemeForest. I love it for the variety. Some pro-designers also recommend Genesis, Thesis, WooThemes and Elegant Themes.

Lead Capture Service

Aweber

It's the market leader in lead capturing and very easy to use. You can start off with a $1 for first month trial plan. Other good options are MailChimp and GetResponse.

Landing Pages

LeadPages

I've just started using their services and I must say that the results have been great. The conversion rate in one of my websites is 65% (that's crazy!). OptinMonster is also a favorite in the internet marketing circle.

Outsourcing Sites

Fiverr

Get all your small tasks done for just $5. I have an entire team of freelancers from Fiverr helping me with various tasks in my business.

Elance

A great place to find all kinds of freelancers. Obviously, it's more expensive than Fiverr, but the quality is also far superior.

Odesk

Very similar to Elance. In fact, both the companies have merged now. I use this site as a backup when I don't find people on Elance.

99Designs

If you have a budget of at least $299 for designing your logo, stationary product label, etc., this is the go-to place. Designers will compete with each other for the job you've posted and you get to choose the best one.

Designing

Canva

If you have no clue about Photoshop (like me!), this site will be a great tool. I make Facebook posts, blog photos, website banners, book covers, etc., on my own using this brilliant online software. PicMonkey is another tool similar to Canva.

Pixlr

This is a great photo-editing software to create some good Photoshop-like effects.

Dollar Photo Club

This is the site I use to buy stock photos. You can buy any photo for just $1. Way cheaper than the other stock photo sites.

Screen Capturing (recommended by Rob Cubbon as well)

Camtasia

I use this software to create screen capture videos for my courses, interviews and blogs. The best software for PC. If you are using a Mac, go for ScreenFlow.

Money Transactions

Paypal

This one is a must use. You'll need it for buying most of the products and services online.

Payoneer

This is a great service, especially for people living outside the U.S. to get their payments as direct deposits instead of checks.

Podcasting Resources (recommended by John Lee Dumas)

Microphones

Logitech ClearChat

Audio-Technica ATR 2100

Heil Sound PR40

Audio Editing Software

Adobe Audition

Audacity

Garageband

Skype call recording software

eCamm Call Recorder for Mac

Pamela for PC

Please Note:

None of the links given in this book are affiliate links.

About The Author

Hi! I am Jyotsna Ramachandran, the HomeEntrepreneur™ (stay-at-home mom + entrepreneur). My journey towards freedom began when I decided never to be an employee ever again.

I tried out various businesses to support my decision - started a staff recruitment agency, became a franchisee of a chocolate brand, did freelance web designing, etc. The arrival of my daughter Advika was the turning point in my life. I realized during my maternity break that none of my businesses were generating income if I was not actively working. I was actually self-employed, I was not a business owner. I had not built in the right systems to automate my businesses. I understood that in order to enjoy true freedom, I needed to create passive income streams. The best way to do that was to start online businesses. I now run a book publishing company called Happy Self Publishing and coach people on how they too can convert their passion into an online business through my website.

You can connect with me in the following ways:

Website:

http://jyotsnaramachandran.com

Email:

jyotsna@jyotsnaramachandran.com

Facebook:

http://facebook.com/jyotsna.entrepreneur

Twitter:

http://twitter.com/jyotsnar

YouTube:

https://www.youtube.com/user/jyotsna0205

Made in the USA
San Bernardino, CA
02 November 2017